Of Men and Dreams

ROBERT BOWNE, 1744-1818, founder of Bowne & Co.

Of Men
and Dreams

The story of the people of Bowne & Co.

and the fulfillment of their dreams

in the company's 200 years

from 1775 to 1975

EDMUND A. STANLEY, JR.

BOWNE & CO., INC.

NEW YORK, NEW YORK

This book is dedicated

TO THE MEN AND WOMEN OF BOWNE & CO.,

whose dreams and dedication have brought the

company through "wars, rumors of wars,

panics and disasters innumerable"

into its third century.

CONTENTS

PREFACE

In an organization that operates night and day under the continual stress of meeting a deadline, opportunities to pause and reflect are few. The days and months slip by almost imperceptibly. So it seems to have been throughout the 200-year history of Bowne & Co.

Until 1950, no known effort had been made to learn of the beginnings of New York's oldest business establishment operating under the same name since its founding. But the author, curious about the old company he had newly joined, began his research and a first edition of this history was published in 1952.

This second edition, published in celebration of the Bicentennial of Bowne & Co., Inc., incorporates material collected over the past twenty years.

We hope that *Of Men and Dreams* will be of interest to our friends and to the hundreds of descendants of Robert Bowne, our founder, who are scattered all over the world.

NEW YORK IN 1775. A British man-of-war lies at anchor, its longboat in the foreground. The steeple of Trinity Church can be seen rising above the surrounding buildings.

1775 ONE FEBRUARY MORNING, in 1775, the merchants along Queen Street (now Pearl Street) were surprised to see the sidewalk in front of No. 39 piled high with casks and boxes and to note, in the window above, a laboriously painted placard which read "Bowne & Co. Merchants."

Unmindful of a light snowfall or their audience, Robert Bowne and his two associates began carrying the merchandise from the walk to the shelves of their new shop. This labor was pleasant indeed to men who, for the past few months, had spent sleepless nights weighing the pros and cons of investing hard-earned savings in this new enterprise, to be launched in the wake of the Townshend Duties, the Boston "Massacre" and "Tea

10

Party," and other events that did not serve to inspire confidence in a bright commercial future for New York City.

However, for these young men the die was cast and they set themselves assiduously to the task of making a success of the business. A newspaper advertisement of the day announced:

Bowne & Co., newly established at No. 39 Queen Street, has for sale Writing Paper, English and American; Account Books; Quills and Pens; Binding and Printing materials; Bolting Cloths; Powder, Furs, Nails, Glass and Dry Goods; Pitch Pine Boards; and a few casks of low-priced Cutlery.

THE STATUE OF KING GEORGE III being pulled down from its pedestal in Bowling Green during the demonstration which followed the news of the Declaration of Independence.

JOHN BOWNE'S HOME, built in 1661, still stands today, a shrine to religious freedom. Here the Quakers met, in defiance of Governor Peter Stuyvesant. Below, the peg-legged governor listens as John Bowne states his case.

Although all this happened about a year and a half before the Declaration of Independence, Robert Bowne was an American of four generations. His great-great-grandfather Thomas Bowne, came from England to Boston in 1649 and then migrated to Flushing, Long Island, where, with his son, John, he purchased farm land from the Matinecock Indians for "eight strings of white wampum" (about fourteen dollars). In 1661 they began construction of the house which still stands today, having been a home for nine generations of the family.

In his memoirs, robust but lame 76-year-old Thomas Bowne records an experience which, for us, 314 years later, seems difficult to imagine happening in one of the boroughs of New York City.

Last evening just at early candlelight, it being quite cool, I thought to walk to the new dwelling. I crossed the turnpike, and had not reached the other side, when a great bear sprang out upon me with such force that I was almost knocked down. I quickly recovered my feet, but the beast was only a few feet away, and for a second my arm seemed paralyzed. Seeing the dreadful creature, his jaws wide open, making ready for another attack, I bethought myself of my good crutch, and stepping quickly forward, thrust it down the bear's throat. Strength was given me at the moment of peril. I stood and looked at him dying, never removing my good stick until he breathed his last.

John Bowne was one of the early defenders of religious freedom in the colonies. Inspired by the simple faith of the Society of Friends, he invited its members to meet in his home. This

13

sect, called "Quakers" because their leader, George Fox, bade a critic "tremble at the word of the Lord," had long been a thorn in the side of New Amsterdam's fiery-tempered governor, Peter Stuyvesant. He had issued an ordinance forbidding their gatherings and at once a warrant went out for John Bowne's arrest. The staunch Quaker not only refused to deny his faith and pay the fine imposed but would not remove his hat in the governor's presence. A prison term brought no change of heart and so Bowne was ordered "transported from the province, as an example to others."

Undaunted, he pleaded his case in Holland, where the court was greatly impressed by his eloquence and, permitting him to return home, instructed Governor Stuyvesant to end persecution of the Society of Friends and to be guided by the principle that "the consciences of men ought ever to remain free and unshackled." On his arrival in New York, John Bowne is said to have met the governor on the street, and, according to a contemporary author, the latter "seemed ashamed and said he was glad to see him home again, a token of repentance, and of ingenuous disposition, such as few, if any, of the rigid, persecutors in New England ever showed."

John Bowne was married three times and had sixteen children. His eldest son, Samuel, was also twice widowed and he raised a family of fifteen. The latter's fifth child by his first wife was John Bowne, whose son, Robert, was to leave the old family home to establish, in 1775, the firm which today bears his name.

14

Bowne & Co. prospered, but in the shadow of uncertainty. On 1776 July 9, 1776, merchants quickly closed their shops and joined the crowds which gathered at the corner of Broad and Wall Streets to hear the reading of a famous document signed five days before at Philadelphia. Reactions were mixed, but many formed a column and marched to Bowling Green where the gilded statue of George III was pulled down from its pedestal.

During the following month General Howe landed some 20,000 British troops on Staten Island and on August 27th attacked and defeated Washington's force of 7,000 at Brooklyn Heights. Demoralized, but still resourceful, the American Army, under cover of darkness and a dense fog, crossed the river to Manhattan. With thousands of other New Yorkers, the Bownes, and their infant daughter, fled in the wake of this defeat.

Robert Bowne, a Quaker and successful merchant, was not altogether sympathetic to the cause of the "Revolution." His religious scruples forbade violence as a means of resolving conflict and, from a business standpoint, he could see only economic chaos as the result of the struggle. The following letter, written at the home of his father-in-law, gives us some insight into his sentiments:

SHREWSBURY, N. J.
DECEMBER 3RD, 1776

Dear Brother,

I have long waited for a good opportunity to write thee, as I make no doubts you are anxious to hear how it fares with us in this time of general calamity. As yet we have been much favored

15

in every respect. The 27th of last month Betsy was safely deliv-
ered of a fine son, Robert Hartshorne Bowne. I have endeav-
ored to avoid giving offense to any and have associated with very
few persons here, finding it much the best thing to do. There are
many of quick temper about who seem bent on driving out
anyone who does not approve of these violent and unjust pro-
ceedings. We New Yorkers have been repeatedly threatened.

Joseph Thorne has been down here several times this Fall.
We have contrived matters in the best manner we were capable
of to avoid suffering by the depreciation of the Continental
currency. The last time he was here, about two weeks ago, he
brought 1500 Dollars, which, seeing no prospect of laying out
to advantage in these parts, we concluded best for him to go
down to Virginia and lay out the amount in Tobacco and wait
until matters are settled, which we hope will not be long.

I am just informed that some of the King's Troops and Light
Horse are nine to ten miles this side of Amboy. Consequently
the Provincials have withdrawn the guards from along the shore
and given me this opportunity of writing thee.

Thy affectionate Brother,

ROBT. BOWNE

Though Robert Bowne's letter might lead us to think of him as a Tory, this was not the case. Factors already noted shaped his views at the outset, but soon he, and most of his friends, began to partake of the vision of a new and free nation. His subsequent letters reflect this change of heart and his deeds, yet to be described, bear it out.

With the cessation of hostilities and Washington's triumphant 1783 celebration at Fraunces Tavern, those who had fled began to return to their city. The havoc wrought by war had been great. Two fires had swept much of the district below Wall Street and many found charred and silent ruins where their homes had been. On the site of the first fire, a cluster of shanties called "Canvas Town" had sprung up, populated by deserters from both armies, underworld characters, and derelicts. Hundreds of unemployed begged on the streets. Crime and lawlessness went unchecked since the prisons were crowded to overflowing, mostly with debtors, many owing less than ten dollars.

However, the citizens of New York were an industrious lot and as Spring approached, the ruins were cleared, new houses and shops erected, and trade slowly revived.

A DIFFICULT DECISION

In the succeeding years Bowne & Co. increased its sale of stationery supplies and began to do printing work. In one respect this development saddened Robert Bowne, because one of his most promising young associates, whose interests lay in another direction, decided to strike out on his own. With a background of peddling bakery goods from door to door, he started with the company in 1784 at $2 per week, but soon amazed his new employer with his industry and ready grasp of the business. He handled what fur trade the firm had and made a few trips into the wilderness, gaining the friendship of many of the trappers and even learning the rudiments of the Mohawk and Seneca languages. On his return from a trip to Montreal, he tried to persuade Robert Bowne to devote all the capital of the company to this growing and profitable business, but after careful consideration, the latter declined. The young man's name was John Jacob Astor.

Over a hundred years later, on the site of the headquarters of Astor's fur operations in Michilimachinac, Michigan, excavation for a new building uncovered a battered silver watch of the English bull-dog style. Still legible on the back was the inscription "Presented to John Jacob Astor by R. Bowne, 1785."

EIGHTEENTH CENTURY PRINT SHOP

Since the time of Johann Gutenberg and the invention of movable type, some three hundred years before, the advances in printing methods had been few indeed. In Bowne & Co. and the other establishments of the city, all the type was of course set by hand. Between impressions, the type was inked by means of a leather bag filled with ink-soaked wool. The coarse paper required wetting to insure proper impression and the type was cleaned with lye following use. The hand press used stood over seven feet high and took a sheet 17 by 22 inches.

Paper and type were imported from England and the accepted costume of the journeyman printer — knee breeches, buckled shoes, and skull cap — harkened back to European traditions. The shops catered to local needs, and, aside from newspapers and pamphlets, produced a great variety of handbills, broadsides, book plates, playbills, and other random pieces.

18

A PRINT SHOP of the late 18th Century. At the left, journeymen compositors are setting type from large wooden cases. In the background, the proprietor and a customer discuss a job. At the right, one pressman inks the type form while the other lifts the printed sheet from the tympan. Behind them, with a pull of the press bar, a sheet is printed.

19

PHILANTHROPY

The business grew and became sufficiently well-established for Robert Bowne to be able to devote some time to philanthropic and other endeavors. Out of the intellectual and spiritual awakening of the times grew the belief in the dignity of the common man and a feeling of social responsibility for those afflicted with ills not of their own making nor within their power to correct.

1784   The plight of black people in the United States had already become the concern of many. Though all blacks brought to America were transported for the purpose of being sold into slavery, by the late 18th Century many had escaped from their masters or had been given their freedom. They sought refuge in the Northern states, but soon found themselves victims of a clever scheme which exploited their former status. Bands of kidnappers would seize unsuspecting blacks, bring them to one of the Southern states, and sell them. Incensed by this inhuman practice and slavery in general, a public meeting was held, and the "Manumission Society" formed, with George Clinton, Alexander Hamilton, Robert Bowne, John Jay, Thomas Eddy and several others, as directors. A prophetic note was struck in their joint resolution:

The Society, viewing with commiseration the poor African slave, will exert all lawful means to ameliorate his sufferings, and ultimately to free him from bondage and to impart to him the benefits of as much education as seems best calculated to fit him for the enjoyment and right understanding of his future privileges and duties when he shall become a free man and citizen.

Soon afterward came partial fulfillment of the Society's aims as a result of laws passed in the state legislature, but the nation, as a whole, was to have more than half a century of slavery before the Emancipation Proclamation of 1863.

ESTABLISHING A FREE SCHOOL

With the return of peace, the population of the city increased rapidly, largely as a result of immigration from Europe. Though certain private and church schools existed, it was apparent that many children were to grow up ignorant of the history, philosophy, and even the language of the new nation. On February 19, 1805, De Witt Clinton, John Pintard, Archibald Gracie, Col. Henry Rutgers, Robert Bowne and a few others met at the home of John Murray, Jr. in Pearl Street to discuss the problem. Colonel Rutgers offered to donate a site for a school house and, thus inspired, the group formed "The Society for Establishing a Free School in the City of New York." The scholars were to be chosen on the basis of need, irrespective of "sect, creed, nationality, or name" and state aid was sought. These were the beginnings of the great free school system of today.

THE NEW YORK HOSPITAL

Chartered by George III in 1771, the Society of the New York Hospital was reorganized after its buildings were destroyed by fire during the Revolutionary War. Robert Bowne held an enviable record of service to this institution which was to grow

21

to become the world-famous New York Hospital-Cornell Medical Center. As a governor for 34 years and its vice president for the last thirteen, he worked at various times with James Duane, Robert Murray, Thomas Eddy, Samuel Franklin, Isaac Roosevelt, and many other prominent figures of the time. Perhaps the most forward looking of these men was Thomas Eddy. This close personal friend of Robert Bowne was a driving force behind almost every philanthropic enterprise. Many years before his theories gained popular acceptance, he advocated penal codes which stressed reeducation rather than punishment and sought special treatment for juvenile delinquents. At a time when the mentally ill, thought to be possessed by devils, were herded into prisons and chained in their cells, he advanced the notion that mental disease was curable and that these unfortunates required medical treatment. Beginning in 1803 the Society set aside some rooms in the hospital for mental patients and in 1817, at a cost of $9,348, acquired the 38-acre estate of Gerard De Peyster, where Columbia University now stands, and established the Bloomingdale Asylum, laying the foundation of psychiatric practice and research in this country.

Typical of the hospital's trials and tribulations in those early days is the following incident which took place on April 13, 1788. It was an unseasonably warm Sunday afternoon and a group of boys were playing in the yard behind The New York Hospital. A thrown ball barely missed a second-story window, but in doing so drew attention to a strange object hanging over the sill. On closer inspection it proved to be a human arm. Entranced, if somewhat frightened, one of the boys climbed a

THE NEW YORK HOSPITAL in Robert Bowne's time and today.

nearby tree which provided an excellent view through the window. He saw, to his horror, what seemed to be a man, writhing in pain, while doctors tore him limb from limb. Taking little comfort in the fact that he was witnessing one of the early classes in experimental medicine which utilized cadavers, he jumped down from the tree to report his findings. Terrified, the boys ran out of the yard babbling their story to passersby and soon an angry mob collected at the hospital gates. Explanations fell on deaf ears, and the doctors were forced to flee, ultimately finding refuge under police protection in a nearby jail. Finally the Mayor, and a number of the governors of the hospital, were able to restore order and by the next day physicians were making their normal rounds in comparative safety.

THE HEALTH OF THE CITIZENRY

In 1793, with the yellow fever epidemic raging, Robert Bowne formed the New York City Health Committee and became its first chairman. His first act was to provide a sedan chair, which in those days must have served the combined purpose of stretcher and ambulance, to bring those afflicted to the newly established hospital on the site of what now is Bellevue Hospital.

Dr. Valentine Seaman, in his *Diary and Prescription Book,* notes that on January 11, 1796 he "received of the Health Committee by the hands of Robert Bowne £40 8s. 6d. for services rendered the poor during the late epidemic fever."

The fever subsided and then broke out again. The summer of 1798 was the worst ever, with those who could afford to do so moving from their homes in the city to the country — today's Greenwich Village. More than 2,000 people died. Bank Street in Greenwich Village gets its name from the days of the epidemic when the Bank of New York had its temporary offices and vault there.

In addition to his philanthropic endeavors, Robert Bowne interested himself as well in the commercial needs of the city. As unbelievable as it seems today, Bowne & Co. was established at a time when New York was without a bank, a fire insurance company, or reliable inland transportation.

NEW YORK'S FIRST BANK

On February 24, 1784, a number of prominent business men met at the Merchants' Coffee House to organize the City's first bank — the Bank of New York. Stock subscription books were made available at Bowne & Co. and at several other firms, and the shares were quickly subscribed. At the next meeting, twelve directors were elected, including Alexander Hamilton, Robert Bowne, Samuel Franklin, John Vanderbilt and Isaac Roosevelt. 1784

The bank's first home was in the sitting room of a private residence, the Walton House. Its architectural motif was followed many years later in the board room of the present offices at 48 Wall Street. The house was located across the street from the sugar refinery owned by Isaac Roosevelt, one of the bank's early presidents. Mr. Roosevelt was able to combine the management of the two businesses by going first to the refinery and then crossing the street to the bank in mid-morning!

THE BANK OF NEW YORK at the corner of Wall and William
Streets when Robert Bowne was a director.

At first the bank was not incorporated but later a petition
to incorporate was signed by Robert Bowne and twelve others.
The petition was renewed in 1789, 1790 and 1791, when it
was finally passed by the legislature. The bank then issued
2,000 sheets of circulating notes "struck off on a hand press
in the bank," undoubtedly provided by Bowne & Co.

In 1794 the bank made a loan of $200,000 at 5 per cent

interest to the United States government to help secure protection for shipping from the depredations of Algerian pirates and to ransom American citizens.

The bank's mementos of those early days include the large iron key to the bank used by the Cashier, early checks addressed simply to "The Bank" (there being only one at the time), and Warrant No. 1, which, in effect, was the first United States bond ever issued. Signed by Alexander Hamilton, Secretary of the Treasury, it was for $20,000, part of a total loan of $200,000 which the bank had subscribed for in its entirety in September, 1789.

Today, in the bank's vault, can be found the depositors' ledgers dating back to 1784. They are in perfect condition and all entries are, of course, made in beautiful script. To use current parlance, Bowne & Co. carried a "five-figure" balance, one of the bank's largest accounts.

There are probably few other business relationships in the United States that have been of greater duration than the one that has existed for 191 years between Bowne & Co. and The Bank of New York. Today the bank is transfer agent for Bowne's

THE IRON KEY used by the bank's Cashier at that time.

27

common stock and the bank's annual and interim reports are printed by Bowne.

Robert Bowne was also instrumental in founding the Bank of America (subsequently merged with what is now the First National City Bank of New York), and its first checks, issued in 1810, bear the imprint of Bowne & Co.

'MUTUAL ASSURANCE'

1787   In 1787 most of the group that had given impetus to the founding of the Bank of New York met to organize "The Mutual Assurance Company for Insuring Houses from Loss by Fire in the City of New York." The Society sought to "assure the mutual security of all subscribers and their neighbors and fellow citizens on most equal terms and without view of private or separate gain." Insurance was available to those within a two-mile radius of City Hall and premiums were set according to the risk of the particular trade, the most hazardous being those of the "brewer, cooper or joiner, tavern keeper, tallow chandler, and printer."

THE ERIE CANAL

1791   Today the Erie Canal is something vaguely remembered from history books. It was, however, a significant turning point in the nation's development. The slender thread of water that was eight years in the making reduced the hazardous overland journey from Buffalo to New York City from 20 to 6 days, cut freight rates from $100 to $15 per ton, and stimulated growth of not only the communities along its banks but, more important, the great wilderness beyond the Appalachians.

The canal had its origin in surveys made in the 1780's by an able engineer, better known as a soldier and statesman. George Washington toured the Mohawk and Hudson valleys and concluded that if New York could take advantage of the only gap in the 1,000-mile mountain range which paralleled the Eastern seaboard, it would surely become the "seat of Empire."

Robert Bowne showed a great deal of interest in these surveys and in 1791 helped organize an inland navigation company. His was a modest undertaking, a three-mile canal of five locks near Little Falls, New York, but it proved what might be done on a larger scale. By 1811 a few more successful ventures had given sufficient impetus to the idea to have the governor establish a canal commission "to explore the whole route for inland navigation from the Hudson River to Lake Ontario and to Lake Erie."

One of the tasks of the commission was to seek help from the federal government, but President James Madison, though polite, was unsympathetic. Undaunted, they persuaded the legislature not to abandon the project and in 1817 construction began.

The years that followed were difficult beyond description. The project was too vast to be other than dismissed as visionary by the great majority who regarded the canal as a "big ditch" in which "would be buried the treasures of the state, to be watered by the tears of posterity."

As the canal approached completion, there were many festivities and public meetings. At a large gathering in New York City, Governor De Witt Clinton paid this tribute:

Let me on this occasion discharge a debt of gratitude and of justice to the late Robert Bowne. He is now elevated above human panegyric and reposes, I humbly and fervently believe, in the bosom of his God. He had at an early period devoted his attention to this subject and was master of all its important hearings. To his wise counsels, intelligent views and patriotic exertions, we were under incalculable obligations. I never left the society of this venerable man without feeling the most powerful inducements for the most animated efforts.

Finally, in 1825, at a cost of $7,000,000 the Erie Canal became a reality. A water channel, forty feet wide and four feet

THE CELEBRATION in New York harbor marking the opening of the Erie Canal on November 4, 1825.

A SCENE along the Canal. Tandem horses draw the flat-bottomed boat.

deep, now spanned the 350 miles between Buffalo and Albany, where it met the Hudson River. In its first year of operation this slender thread of water carried 10,000 barges. Cities mushroomed along the canal banks, real estate values soared, and New York was indeed the "Empire State".

THE ROLE OF THE MERCHANT

Despite Robert Bowne's many philanthropic endeavors and the responsibilities of his company's growing printing and sta-

31

tionery business, he and his sons were general merchants and their role in the commercial life of the city and nation was a complex and fascinating one.

In the days before the typewriter and copying machine, all correspondence was written by hand and each letter had to be copied by hand for the company's records. We are very fortunate that The New-York Historical Society, in its Manuscript Room, has the letter books of Bowne & Co. for 1807-1808 and 1817-1823.

These letter books show the Bownes performing many business functions, each of which is now the province of distinct and specialized firms. They dealt in a variety of goods and services. They acted as agents for other merchants, speculated in land, bought and sold commodities such as wheat, flour, wine, brandy, rum, cloth and potash, and provided banking services such as advancing credit to clients, issuing notes, and discounting the notes of others.

Because there was no uniform currency in the United States until the second half of the 19th Century, commercial transactions differed markedly from current practice. Of central importance to early 19th Century business was the system of notes and discounting. Notes, or checks as they are now known, were not always transmitted directly from creditor to payee. Indeed, third, fourth and fifth party notes were not uncommon. This practice was necessary because of the lack of an adequate circulating medium and, for all practical purposes, the absence of banking laws of any kind. The only restraining and quasi-regulatory agency was the Bank of the United States. This agency of the national government, newly organized under the federal constitution, was one of the important measures urged by Alexander Hamilton, first Secretary of the Treasury, in developing the powers of the new government. The bank's charter ran for 20 years, but political opposition and ineffective organization of the bank's supporters prevented its renewal. With the demise of the bank in 1811, the United States plunged into a period of war and lack of fiscal controls.

ROBERT BOWNE AND HIS FAMILY

To Robert Bowne and to the Society of Friends, of which he was a loyal member, a man's family was of fundamental importance. He had nine children and fifty grandchildren and today there are a number of collections of letters which give us wonderful insight into the close family ties that existed.

In the collection in the Manuscript Room of the Columbia University Library, we find this letter from Robert Bowne to the boarding school teacher of his youngest son, William.

Esteemed Friend,

Thine of the 3rd Instant I duly rec'd. It is a great satisfaction to hear so favourable an acct of our dear William. He is naturally of a good disposition and manageable, but from his lively disposition and great activity, he wants a watchfull care continually over him. He mentions in a letter to Asher Corlies that he and another Boy hired a ship, went out a sailing and came near to oversetting, in which case they might have been

drowned. I am more apprehensive of danger in his having suf-
fered to go on the river in·small boats & on the ice. And hope
thee will be particularly careful how thee allows them in these
practices. I wish thee to encourage and keep William to his
studies as much as possible. What ever further clothing he may
stand in need of and a small supply of pocket money as thee may
think proper, I must request thee to furnish him with. I now send
by Isaac Sharples $67 which pays up thy acct to the 15th of last
month. The 17 cents over thee will please hand over to William
as coming from me. And remember his Mother's and my dear
love to him and tell him its our earnest desire he does not ex-
pose himself on the river. Much love in which my wife joins to
thee and thine,

I remain affectionately thy affc.

ROBT. BOWNE

William was 12 years old when this was written. In 1815, when he was 20, his father sent him to Europe to assess business conditions in Holland, Germany, England and Russia and to do some trading. William's papers included a letter from John Ferguson, then Mayor of the City of New York, in which the mayor wrote to request that William be permitted to "pass wheresoever his lawful pursuits may call him, freely and without any molestation, in going, staying and returning, and to give him all the friendly advice and protection as I would in the like case." William also had a very elaborate visa from the vice-consul of "His Imperial Majesty the Emperor of All the Russias to the United States" and he was one of the few visitors to that country.

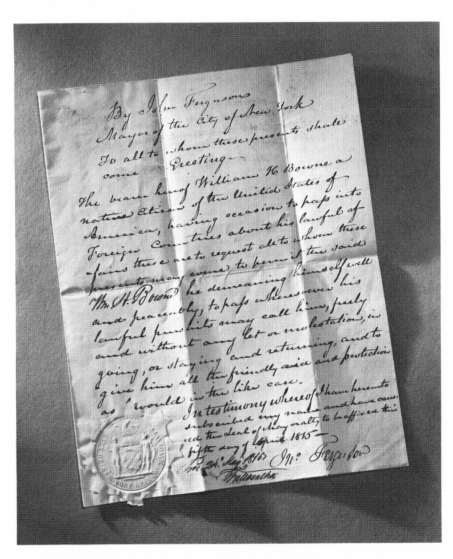

LETTER OF INTRODUCTION written by Mayor John Fergu-
son of New York City for Robert Bowne's son, William, to facilitate
his travel in England, Germany, Holland and Russia on behalf of
Bowne & Co. The mayor's seal appears in the lower left hand corner.

In one of Robert Bowne's last letters to his son, he conveys news of the family and then turns to business:

I hope before this reaches thee, thou will have received the proceeds of the ivory. Should it still be on hand, inform thyself of the price it will bring in Moscow. I am told there is canal navigation the greater part of the way from Archangel to that city, where there is the best prospect of its selling to advantage. Should it be transported it would be necessary to have all the small teeth put in carts or sacks, as there will be great danger of their being lost by the way. Let them be sold for what they will bring, and my half of the proceeds, shouldst thou not have occasion for it, thou mayst invest in sheetings or duck as the most certain articles, though shouldst thou meet with any articles which may promise far greater profits, thou art at liberty to try small amounts.

Later in the letter Robert Bowne comments on the banking situation at home:

A considerable embarrassment attends our trade for want of a circulating medium that the people can have confidence in. The multiplying of State banks have ruined the credit of their paper. Congress, I expect, will be under the necessity of establishing a national bank or issuing small treasury notes to be a legal tender and the specie is continually going out and little or none coming in.

One can sense how much confidence Robert Bowne must have had in his son and how proud he must have been of this young man who, as a youngster was worrying his father by going out on the river in a small boat. What a terrible blow it must have been when Robert Bowne received the news that on his voyage home from Russia, William was suddenly taken ill and died at sea less than a month after his twenty-first birthday.

From the Bible record of Robert Bowne we have this report of that sad event:

Our very dear and tenderly beloved son William departed from this life on board the ship Lady Galatin, *Captain Swain, on his return voyage from St. Petersburg in Russia on the 24th day of the 10th month in 1816. From his sweet and amiable deportment during his illness, the captain and ship's company became so much attached to him that they were induced to endeavor to preserve his precious remains and return them to his greatly afflicted parents which they were enabled to effect to our great consolation, and he was interred in Friends burial ground on the 15th of 11th month in 1816, attended by a large number of friends and the captain and seamen belonging to the ship.*

A LOSS KEENLY FELT

In celebrating the completion of the Erie Canal, Governor De 1818
Witt Clinton spoke of the "late" Robert Bowne. Death came to the founder of Bowne & Co. on February 7, 1818, and as can be appreciated from an acquaintance with the scope of his endeavors, his loss was keenly felt by persons in all walks of life. Thomas Eddy wrote a simple but heartfelt obituary about "a man of great benevolence" whose "active mind, open purse, expanded heart, and willing feet knew no bounds."

The years following the War of 1812 were prosperous ones and Robert H. Bowne and John L. Bowne carried on their father's business with considerable financial success. John Bowne, in 1824, retired from the firm to become the first president of the United States Fire Insurance Company and held this post until his death in 1847. By today's standards his lofty position may not seem too enviable. Office hours for the company were from "8 o'clock a.m. to sunset every day, the first day of the week excepted only" and the president's salary was set at "fifteen hundred dollars per annum."

Robert H. Bowne married Sarah Hartshorne and purchased a sizable farm near his wife's home in Rahway, New Jersey. A replica of the certificate recording their marriage in 1807 now hangs in the offices of Bowne & Co. It was engrossed by hand and then signed by the 61 witnesses to the traditional Quaker ceremony. They had seven children, whose letters from school are a little unfamiliar in their language but not in their subject matter:

LINDLEY'S SCHOOL
MAY 12TH, 1831

Dear Mother,

The good old fashioned days when dutiful and loving sons wrote long letters to their affectionate parents appear to have gone by, but I trust thee will believe that I appreciate thy sympathy and interest in all that concerns me, and feel more and more there is no friend like a mother, without my multiplying words to try to convince thee of it.

I would have answered thy letter on seconday last or before but I am in the midst of the review of all my lessons preparing for the examination which will begin a week hence.

Aunt Jane often visits us and with her characteristic liberality furnishes us with eatables of various kinds which I assure thee are most acceptable.

Please give my love to all and tell Father I should prefer his telling me if my letters are not written plain enough instead of the Headmaster.

Thy loving son,

WILLIAM

SHORT-LIVED OPTIMISM

Prosperity for New York and comparative freedom from strife in the country as a whole continued, and despite record cold weather for December, 1835, a happy Christmas and New Year were anticipated by all. But this optimism was short-lived.

At about 9:00 p.m. on December 16th, with the temperature well below the zero mark, a small fire broke out in the dry-goods store of Comstock & Adams on Beaver Street. The flames soon engulfed the neighboring buildings and as the heat became more intense, new copper roofs and iron shutters became red hot and molten copper began falling in drops like rain on the pavement. The fire brigades, tired from battling a blaze the previous night, arrived to find the hydrants frozen solid. When water was sought from the river it promptly froze in buckets and pipes. A strong gale blew up and the monster raced toward the East River, where a brig, loaded with kegs of gunpowder from the Brooklyn Navy Yard, was making a hazardous crossing to provide for the dynamiting of a fire-break.

When, three days later, the last flames had died down, most of downtown New York — 17 blocks and 570 buildings — was reduced to a charred and smoking ruin.

The famous diarist and Mayor of New York City, Philip Hone, made this entry in his diary on December 17th: "How shall I record the events of last night, or how attempt to describe the most awful calamity which has ever visited the United States? I am fatigued in body, disturbed in mind, and my fancy filled with images of horror which my pen is inadequate to describe."

Once the fire was over, looting was a serious problem. Hone, a little self-righteously, comments as follows. "I have been alarmed by some of the signs of the times which this calamity has brought forth: the miserable wretches who prowled about in the ruins, and became beastly drunk on the champagne and other wines and liquors with which the streets and wharves were lined, seemed to exult in the misfortune, and such expressions were heard as 'Ah! They'll make no more five per cent dividends!'."

Bowne & Co., at 71 Wall Street, was destroyed. Almost every New York insurance firm went into bankruptcy, one business after another failed, and the task of rebuilding was reminiscent of the post-Revolutionary War days.

On the heels of the "Great Fire" came President Jackson's withdrawal of government funds from the Bank of the United

THE GREAT FIRE OF 1835 as seen from the roof of the Bank of America. The columned building is the old Merchants' Exchange (now the site of the First National City Bank). Bowne & Co., located one block East at 71 Wall Street, was burned to the ground.

41

States in Philadelphia, resulting in a period of paper money, increased cost of living, labor unrest, and finally the financial panic of 1837. Some of the oldest firms failed and a run on the banks brought about suspension of specie payment.

THE FIRST AMERICAN WORLD'S FAIR

By 1840 New York had almost recovered from the two catastrophes and Bowne & Co., located in its new building at the corner of Wall, Pearl, and Beaver Streets was doing well. An advertisement and several invoices from this period show the company to have gained particular prominence in the manufacture of leather-bound account books.

THE MEDAL won by Bowne & Co. in the "Exhibition of the Industry of All Nations" at the first American World's Fair. The award was for excellence in the manufacture of leather-bound account books.

The Summer of 1853 witnessed the opening of the nation's first World's Fair in "the beautiful Crystal Palace on Murray Hill." On the opening day, President Pierce, having arrived at Battery Park by warship from Washington, rode on horseback up Broadway "through lines of cheering throngs, flag-decked buildings, and welcoming banners."

To the Crystal Palace most of the countries of the world had sent samples of their manufactures for the "Exhibition of the Industry of All Nations." Horace Greeley's *Tribune* described the many displays to be seen and in reporting on the Bookbinding Section observed that "the ledgers for the Bank of New York and the Chemical Bank, in full Russia, and most excellently finished, are particularly good specimens of workmanship."

A CERTIFICATE printed by Bowne & Co. in 1858. Forerunner of today's corporation stock certificate, it entitled the owner to a share in the profits for that particular year.

These ledgers, together with samples of color printing, had been exhibited by Bowne & Co., and earned for the firm the medal of the Fair.

In this day of microfilmed records and complex business machines, it is hard to believe that at one time all records were made in labored Spencerian script in great ledger books of the type once manufactured by Bowne & Co. These volumes, furnished with sheets of handmade paper imported from England and bound in the finest Russia — a smooth, dark red leather produced by careful tanning and dyeing — are still to be found in the archives of many of the banks.

In addition to its thriving account book business, Bowne & Co. did a variety of printing work. Today, in the company archives, are to be found such pieces as "By-laws of the Independent Base Ball Club, embracing the Rules and Regulations as adopted by the National Association of Base Ball Players," "A Hand Book of Streets and Distances, showing The Length, and Intermediate Distance from Street to Street, of all the Streets in the City of New York" and "An Ordinance for the Licensing and Otherwise Regulating the Use and Employment of Carts and Cartmen, Dirt Carts and Dirt Cartmen, and Public Porters, and For the Preserving of Good Order in the City of New York."

Some of them make rather entertaining reading today. Bowne's copy of the first rules of organized baseball was owned by A. G. Spalding and his signature appears on the second page. Included among the rules is one that states that "Any member who shall be inebriated when at a meeting of business, or at a

PIECES PRINTED BY BOWNE & CO. in the years before the Civil War. What the company looked like in those days can be seen by turning to the end papers of this book where a woodcut, still in the company's possession, is reproduced showing Bowne & Co. at the corner of Wall, Pearl and Beaver Streets. Note the cobblestone street, the stationery wares displayed and the hoist which served to bring goods to and from the floors above.

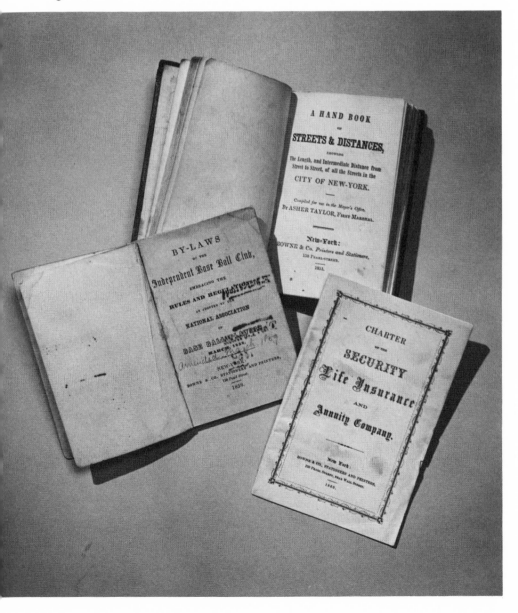

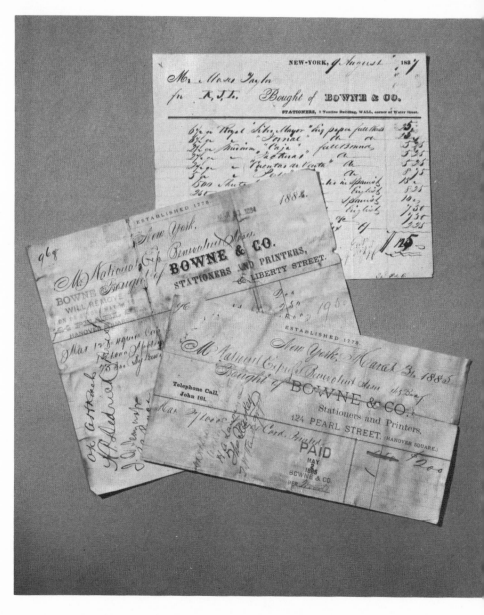

BOWNE & CO. bills from the 1800's. Note that one has apparently been marked down from $250 to $200. On the same bill appears the company's telephone number, John 161.

time when assembled for field exercise, shall be fined one dollar; and on repetition of the same shall be subject to expulsion." Another warns that "Members, when assembled for field exercise, who shall use profane or improper language, shall be fined ten cents for each offence, to be paid before leaving the field."

In the 1850's the three principals of the firm were Robert, William, and John Bowne, all grandsons of the founder, Robert H. Bowne having died in Rahway in 1843. He left his estate to his wife, Sarah, but asked that his "executors exercise discretion with saving such part of it as is now in the hands of Bowne & Co. of New York so that his sons which are his partners in said firm may not be the sufferers by having the capital left in by him too speedily withdrawn."

MR. DEWEY REMINISCES

In the latter part of the 19th Century the historical record 1870 shifts from letters, wills, advertisements and the like to verbal reminiscences of some of the people in the firm. From the company's fifth president, Stanley M. Dewey, we learn that after the death of John and William Bowne, their cousin, Robert, carried on the business alone during the eventful Civil War period. He had three sons and hoped that at least one would succeed him. However, to the great sorrow of the old gentleman, they evidenced neither the requisite inclination nor ability and so, in the person of Mr. Dewey, Robert Bowne

47

found someone who could carry on the firm's traditions if not the family name.

Stanley Dewey was tall, thin, wore a goatee and often a frock coat. A kind, soft-spoken person of high standards, he was generous, but at the same time frugal. He obtained his eyeglasses from a vendor with a cart on Broad Street. He would hold various lenses up to his eye until he had a pair which seemed to give proper vision. These, and a frame, he bought at a cost of 30 cents and they would serve until lost or broken. He worked hard at his business, but still found time to sing in his church choir, teach Sunday school, and do considerable settlement work.

Near the turn of the century, much of the firm's business was in the stationery line and Mr. Dewey would visit the banks and insurance companies downtown, note their requirements as to ink, quills, sealing wax, account books, letterheads, and the like, and return to the office and write up the order. In his reminiscences he recalls crossing the East River by ferry, watching the Brooklyn Bridge under construction, and seeing the New York skyline when Trinity Church was still the tallest building downtown.

He witnessed the change from crank and foot power to steam in operating the printing presses and remembers with what fascination he watched illustrations being cut by hand in boxwood long before the introduction of photoengraving. He notes that Bowne & Co. was one of the first firms to install the telephone though Mr. Bowne would never use it, considering the contrivance "an indecorous way to conduct business affairs."

48

STANLEY M. DEWEY, 1854-1941, became senior partner of
Bowne & Co. in 1898 and then the company's president in 1909
when it incorporated. He retired as president in 1922 but continued
as chairman of the board until his death in 1941.

49

What he terms "one of the more unusual demands" was made of Bowne & Co. one Friday afternoon. The firm had to set up a full-sized press in the offices of one of the banks and have a foreman and pressman on hand Monday morning to imprint a large quantity of bonds which could not be taken out of the customer's possession. He remembers that "at this time we had no cost system and I hardly think there were many in existence in the trade. The foreman merely put on what he considered a fair price for the work done, with the consequence that even when the printing office was very busy, it was likely to show a loss. This state of affairs stimulated my interest in cost systems as against guess work."

'CO-PARTNERSHIP CHANGES'

1898   In November, 1898, on the fiftieth anniversary of his joining the firm, Robert Bowne retired and we find this informative, if occasionally whimsical, report on the editorial page of *The Mercantile & Financial Times*:

Co-partnership changes among well known New York business houses are of continual — it might almost be said of daily — occurrence; and for the most part they do not attract any particular attention, and are not referred to save in the most perfunctory fashion in the columns of the public newspapers.

But once in a while there will be an announcement of a change in connection with a concern of such long and high and honorable standing that it cannot be passed over without special mention — at any rate in the columns of those newspapers that attach more importance to wise and honorable methods in business life than they do to the doings and misdoings of thieves, prize fighters and murderers.

An illustration of what is meant is found in the case of the ancient and honorable house of BOWNE & CO., *printers, blank book manufacturers and stationers, of No. 81, Beaver street.*

Under this style is carried on what is the oldest concern in New York in this line of business — if not in the United States — having been originally founded in 1775 — 123 years ago. On November 1, inst., Mr. Robert Bowne, who had been connected with the firm for more than half a century, retired on account of advancing years, and a new co-partnership was formed on the same day, composed of Mr. Stanley M. Dewey and Mr. Robert J. Lowden, and they will continue the business under the old firm style of Bowne & Co.

Mr. Dewey has been connected with it for thirty years past, and is a thorough master of everything pertaining to the business. He is well and favorably known to the old customers of the house and is looked up to and respected by everybody.

Mr. Lowden entered the house on November 1st, he has a wide and valuable acquaintance here and elsewhere.

Messrs. Bowne & Co. have a well equipped plant at the above address and employ a full force of hands. They do a general printing business, and turn out large quantities of stationery, blank books, etc. They make a specialty of fine work for banks, insurance companies, railroad companies, etc. It can be said

EDMUND A. STANLEY, 1888-1956, joined Bowne in 1908 and
became president in 1922. He headed the firm for 34 years until
his death in 1956.

without exaggeration that there is no concern that does better work than they do, or that enjoys a more honorable reputation.

What an interesting volume it would make if the complete history of this business since the days before the Revolution could be written. Through wars, rumors of wars, panics and disasters innumerable, the house has "calmly pursued the even tenor of its way," to become a veritable Gibraltar of business stability.

After 52 years with the firm, Mr. Dewey sold his interest to a young associate, Edmund A. Stanley, and though retired, paid occasional visits to the plant in the capacity of honorary chairman of the board and respected advisor, until his death at the age of eighty-seven in 1941.

A NEW PRESIDENT

Mr. Stanley, who joined the firm in 1908 and became its sixth 1922
president in 1922, was born in Walsall, England. With the advent of the automobile, his family's saddlery and harness business suffered considerably and so at the age of seventeen he emigrated to the United States. He worked for a while as an errand boy in Newark and then answered an advertisement for a "young man" in a New York newspaper. He entered Mr. Stanley Dewey's office to find a large pile of applications on his desk and a rather stern look on his face. But on being advised of the applicant's name and finding that in school he had excelled in carpentry — a favorite hobby of the old gentleman — quali-

fications were not examined too closely and the young man emerged with a new job.

In 1909 the company was incorporated and showed steady growth during the ensuing years. The plant and offices were moved in 1916 from 81 Beaver Street to 161 Maiden Lane. The firm's traditional work for banking and insurance companies, some of which had its origins many years prior to the memory of anyone in either Bowne & Co. or the customers' employ, was supplemented as the needs of the financial district dictated. For many years the company printed a substantial portion of the securities offering circulars of New York underwriters and, with the inception of the Securities and Exchange Commission in 1933, began specializing in meeting the exacting demands of underwriters, attorneys, and corporations responsible for complying with its requirements.

The Depression of the 1930's was a very difficult time for the company, with many of its customers reducing advertising and promotional budgets to an absolute minimum. Annual sales averaged about $300,000 and in a number of years losses were sustained.

BOWNE & CO., INC. TODAY

In the 1940's business began to improve and in 1946 the sales of the company exceeded $1 million for the first time. During World War II many employees were in the services and the pressure on the remaining crew was great. For a number of weeks at the beginning of the war, the company worked around the

54

THE TWO STANLEYS, whose Bowne tenure has spanned 67 years, are shown at their desks. Mr. Stanley, Sr., in his office at 81 Beaver Street in 1911, was 23 years old. Mr. Stanley, Jr., in his office at 345 Hudson Street in 1969, was 45 years old.

clock printing the application blanks for the purchase of Defense Bonds.

A number of years ago the company's first linotype operator, Philip Lipman, reminisced about his early days with Bowne. "For Mr. Stanley," he writes, "type, paper and ink were as paint, canvas and brush to the artist. He could take the most crude copy and make something out of it. He would call me into his office, sit me down next to his desk and go over the copy line for line telling me what he wanted. 'We'll put this in italic,' he would say, pointing with his pencil, and marking it, 'and this line in even small caps' and so on and invariably the page would turn out to be very handsome even though in the beginning it seemed hopeless."

Another old timer, Carl Riegelhaupt, the pressroom foreman for many years, recalls Mr. Stanley telephoning him at home on a Sunday morning about opening the plant that afternoon to set and print a job which had to be delivered on Monday morning. He, in turn, had to get in touch with Robert McCarthy, plant manager. The two men were neighbors in Greenwich Village and Riegelhaupt, who was Jewish, knew that McCarthy, who was Catholic, would be in church. When McCarthy, in the middle of the service, saw Riegelhaupt genuflect and sit down in the pew opposite him, he knew that the explanation must be a problem at Bowne rather than a change in his colleague's religion.

1949   In 1949 and 1950 two young men, who today are the company's chairman of the board and its president, joined Bowne. Edmund A. Stanley, Jr. had served in the Infantry in combat

56

EDMUND A. STANLEY, JR., born in 1924, came to Bowne in 1949 and was elected a vice president in 1953. When his father died in 1956, he became president and held that post until 1974. He is the chairman of the board of directors of the company and its chief executive officer.

in Belgium and France in World War II and, after graduating from Princeton, came to work for his father and for Bowne. At the time there was an age gap of about 20 years between him

VICTOR SIMONTE, JR., born in 1933, came to work for Bowne in 1950 as a helper in the composing room. He rose through the ranks and in 1974 was elected president of the company.

and the next youngest employee in sales and management and he found it a little frustrating not to be given any work to do that seemed important. But this changed in time and in 1953 he became a vice president, and in 1956, when his father died, he was elected president. In 1974 he resigned this post, but continues as chairman of the board and chief executive officer.

Victor Simonte, Jr., whose father worked as a paper cutter for Bowne, came to work as a helper in the composing room at the age of 17. He rose through the ranks as an apprentice, journeyman, foreman and then plant superintendent. In February, 1967, he was elected vice president for manufacturing and in the fall of that year he attended the Program for Management Development at Harvard Business School. In 1968 he became president of Bowne's New York financial printing company and in 1974 was elected president of the parent company.

From 1927 to 1961 Bowne & Co., Inc. was located at 163 Front Street, close to New York's financial district. In the late 1950's its quarters became increasingly inadequate as sales grew from $1 million in 1950 to $2.4 million in 1960.

In 1961, during a Fall weekend when everyone worked 1961 around the clock, all of the plant equipment was moved to 345 Hudson Street to a single floor of over an acre in size as contrasted to four floors in the old building, with each floor one-eighth the size of that in the new location. New equipment, unmatched customer service facilities, and the latest in communications systems helped to bring Bowne from third place rank in sales among financial printers to first place in the ensuing years and it holds that rank today.

Since 1961, the company has enjoyed the most rapid growth in its history, with sales increasing from $3 million to over $38 million in fiscal 1974.

In 1966 Bowne acquired Garber-Pollack Co. Inc., a trade bindery. In 1968, concurrent with making a first public offering of its common stock, the company acquired The La Salle Street Press, Inc., the largest financial printer in Chicago. Since then, financial printing companies have been started or acquired in Boston, Houston, Los Angeles, and San Francisco.

Bowne has diversified and expanded its efforts to encompass many aspects of word management and document building. The Bowne Family now includes Bowne Time Sharing, Inc., which provides computer text editing services nationwide, and Legal Systems, Inc., a company devoted to servicing the document preparation needs of attorneys. Redler, Inc. designs and produces merchandising aids. Intergraphic Technology, Inc. uses the "cold type" method to produce corporate, textbook, and commercial printing. The six financial printing companies in six major financial centers have compatible typesetting and printing equipment, and are linked by a facsimile transmission network.

THE ROBERT BOWNE FOUNDATION

In 1968, the Robert Bowne Foundation, Inc. was organized. It honors the company's founder whose "active mind, open purse, expanded heart, and willing feet knew no bounds." The foundation concerns itself chiefly with the disadvantaged in urban areas and has helped to fund many worthwhile projects.

As this is written, the South Street Seaport Museum in New York, with funds provided by the foundation and Edmund A.

BOWNE & CO. PRESSROOMS contrasted. Above, No. 2 Kelly presses at 163 Front Street about 1958. They printed eight pages of a prospectus at 2,000 impressions an hour. Below, the new Mark II Hantcho web press, which prints 64 pages at 20,000 impressions per hour. The new press is the equivalent of 80 of the old presses.

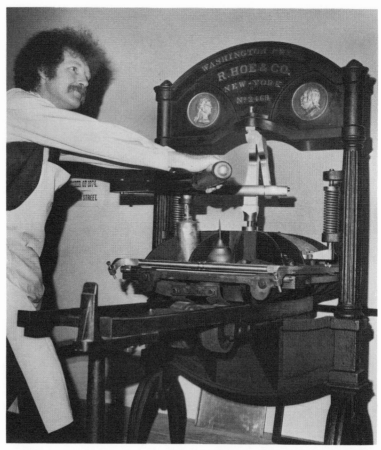

NEW YORK POST PHOTOGRAPH BY TERENCE MC CARTEN

EVENTS OF BOWNE'S BICENTENNIAL are pictured above and on the page opposite. Above, Roger Campbell, director of the Bowne & Co. stationery and printing shop restoration at South Street Seaport Museum in New York, pulls the press bar of the shop's Washington press on opening day, November 13, 1974. Opposite, Paul Vincze, world famous sculptor medallist, works in his studio in Chelsea, London, to complete the plaster model of the Bowne Bicentennial medal. Both sides of the finished medal are shown at right.

PHOTOGRAPH BY JOHN BIGNELL, LONDON

Stanley, Jr., is completing restoration of a building at 211 Water Street that will in many ways duplicate Bowne & Co. in the 1850's. Here visitors to the Seaport from all over the world can see a printing shop in operation as part of a restoration project which encompasses ships at piers and many blocks of shops and exhibits reminiscent of the days of wooden ships and iron men.

LOOKING BACK

1975　Today, as Bowne begins its third century, we look back over our 200-year history and sometimes wonder if in that history we have an asset or a liability. A smugness and trust in the forces of inertia would certainly be a liability, but for us innovation has always been the watchword. In the heritage and the example of those who have gone before lies, we believe, an incentive to attainment and a mandate of responsibility which must be counted a great asset indeed.

COAT OF ARMS of the Bowne family.

ANOTHER STORY

Another story remains to be told. This book has attempted to
give some insight into the life and times of Robert Bowne and
the firm he founded. However, it tells but little of his family.
Robert and Elizabeth Bowne had nine children, fifty grandchildren and 112 great-grandchildren. Hundreds of their descendants are alive today, some of them in the eighth generation. Following are brief sketches of three of Robert Bowne's grandchildren.

ROBERT BOWNE (1825-1906)

Grandson and namesake of the company's founder, Robert Bowne was the last of the family to be active in Bowne & Co. A few people alive at the time of the first edition of this history in 1952 remembered him. One octogenarian, then in his teens, pictured him as a "kindly, soft-spoken Quaker gentleman, who showed more deference to a young man than was the custom of someone at his age and station."

Robert Bowne was born in New York City on June 5, 1825, the son of John L. and Elizabeth (Howland) Bowne. His father had left Bowne & Co. a year earlier to become the first president of the United States Fire Insurance Company. His mother came from a family that had received world renown in the shipping business and were to receive even greater notoriety when the death of Hetty Howland (Wilkes) Green, in 1916, set in motion the most extensive search for missing heirs in the annals of law.

Robert had two brothers and six sisters. One brother died at the age of five and the other at the age of thirty-eight, unmarried. One of his sisters married, one died as a child, and the other four were spinsters, who died at an average age of 84 years.

In 1848, when he was 23, Robert came to work for Bowne & Co., then located at the corner of Wall, Pearl, and Beaver Streets. On April 12, 1860, he married Anna Frances Willis. He was 35 and she, 26. On her mother's side, Mrs. Bowne was the granddaughter of Thomas Cock, famous New York surgeon of the early 19th Century. In the first six years of married life she bore her husband three sons, Robert Jr., Edward and Howland. She had no other children and soon developed an undiagnosed illness.

In an effort to find a climate suited to his wife's health, Robert moved from New York to Elizabeth, New Jersey. In 1876 he took Anna to Savannah and in 1881 she died at the age of 47 in Camden, Maine.

Thus, at the age of 56, Robert Bowne found himself a widower with three sons in their teens, four spinster sisters to look after, and head of a fine old business that was still doing well, but was by no means as successful as it had been in the days of his father and grandfather.

In 1875 Bowne & Co. had celebrated its 100th Anniversary. Certainly the prospects for continuance of the firm and the family name seemed assured. Robert had three fine young sons all of whom could have continued in their father's footsteps. However, this was not to be the case.

Robert Bowne, Jr. was born on February 6, 1861, three days before Jefferson Davis was elected president of the Confederate States of America. Called "Bert," he looked like his mother and grew up to be her favorite. He was an extremely gifted boy and resolved to enter the medical profession, in which his great-grandfather, Thomas Cock, had so distinguished himself.

Robert graduated second in his class at medical school, but was quite chagrined at having missed being first by two points. He was highly thought of by the famous surgeon, Dr. David H. Agnew (1818-1892), and the latter suggested that Robert become his associate in a few years. The position was not immediately open to him because the surgeon felt that his age and youthful appearance might be difficult for patients to accept.

Dismayed at this turn of events, Robert and a young friend decided they would take a trip around the world, a project financed by his mother and doting aunts. In his medical school days Robert had experimented with a new drug called cocaine, even going so far as to give himself injections. In China he became curious about opium and, by the time he returned home, had become an incurable addict. The nature of the addiction and its cure were a mystery in those days and the young man's condition grew worse and worse until his death in 1899 at the age of 38 in California.

Robert Bowne's second son, Edward Willis Bowne, was born on July 20, 1862, and was the namesake of his maternal grandfather. Edward was fond of the outdoors and of his independence, and it would appear that he and his father had little in common. After graduating from Stevens College, in Hoboken, he went West, and braving the threat of hostile Indians and severe climate, bought some land in Colorado and raised horses. Here he suffered an injury which left him somewhat lame for the rest of his life. He returned to New York and in 1905 made his home in Tarrytown, New York. During World War I he was employed as a buyer and shipper of horses for the French government. On one trip, accompanying a load of horses, a German submarine torpedoed the boat off the Spanish coast and captured it. Edward and the others aboard were permitted to take to lifeboats and were set adrift off the coast where they were found, taken ashore, and sent home in an American vessel.

After the war, at the age of 56, Edward Bowne returned to Tarrytown living a rather curious bachelor existence. He was a yachting enthusiast, a familiar figure at the local boat club, and owned several boats over the years, the last one being a 30-foot cruiser. He was something of an expert on antiques and New York history, and had quite a collection of paintings, china, lace, furniture, and what the appraisers of his estate termed "junk." He had a fine set of carpenter's tools and added this skill to his other hobbies.

It would appear that Edward Bowne was gradually exhausting his capital, which consisted principally of his inheritance from the Hetty Green estate. In his declining years he lived in a small furnished room at 85 North Washington Street.

He died in this room on December 14, 1936, at the age of 74 without leaving a will. In his room were found twelve old pictures, three ancient clocks, the usual furniture, many books, a chest of tools, and 74 cents in cash on his dresser. He had no bank account and owned no securities. In his landlord's garage was a car which a wrecker charged $10 to cart away, and in a storage warehouse were fifteen locked trunks, four wooden chests, seven sealed barrels, eleven oil paintings, and some furniture. The court appointed his cousin, Arthur C. Scott, as administrator, and, at auction, his property brought enough to pay funeral and estate expenses.

It is a sad and curious thing that Bowne & Co. and Edward Willis Bowne apparently never contacted one another. In addition to an interest in and knowledge of New York history, he seemed to have kept anything which came his way. We shall never know what memorabilia of Bowne & Co. could have been found in those trunks, chests, and barrels since they and their contents were quickly disposed of by people anxious to settle the estate of an eccentric old man without close friends or relatives.

Howland Bowne was born on November 5, 1866, and named for his paternal grandmother, Elizabeth (Howland) Bowne. At about 20 years of age he was taken on as a clerk in Busk & Jevons, American agents for the Lamport & Holt steamship line which had its head office in Liverpool. The firm was located in the old Produce Exchange building. We may perhaps surmise that in keeping with a custom of the day, it was thought a good idea to see how a boy could make out on his own, prior to his entering the family business.

However, Howland demonstrated little promise of success and gradually his heavy drinking became a problem. On this account the firm was forced to discharge him in the late 1890's. Chagrined and perhaps reluctant to turn to his father, he followed the example of his brother, went to the West, and took up a homestead. In those days the U.S. Government, anxious to settle the new territory, offered free land to settlers who would be willing to hold and farm it for a certain length of time.

But this arduous life was too much for him. Tuberculosis that had been incipient became fully apparent and he entered a hospital in Arizona. In the hospital he met a fellow patient by the name of Elizabeth Fisher, fell in love, and when they were discharged in 1905, they were married.

The couple returned East and with the little money they inherited from his father, bought a house and a small chicken farm

70

in Bound Brook, New Jersey. Because of their health, the doctor at the hospital in Arizona had strongly advised against their having children. However, Elizabeth Bowne soon became pregnant. As was almost to be expected, her child was born dead and she died in childbirth on December 7, 1907, at the age of 36.

Broken in spirit and health, Howland Bowne lost interest in his little business and, in the wake of the financial panic of 1907, was forced to liquidate it. He then sold his house and moved to a small hotel, where he soon was running behind in paying his bills. He was forced to leave the hotel and he had no recourse but to enter the poorhouse.

In 1916, after several years there, he received a communication from a firm of attorneys who advised him that he was a legatee under the trust created by Sylvia Ann Howland. When Miss Howland died in 1865, she gave her niece, Hetty Howland Robinson (who was to marry and become the notorious Hetty Green), half of her valuable property, with the provision that it should ultimately pass to the lineal descendants, by right of representation, of the former's grandfather, Gideon Howland. In 1865 the proviso would not have been difficult to fulfill, but by 1916, when Mrs. Hetty H. R. Green died, the settlement of the million-dollar trust — which involved one of the most thorough genealogical compilations in history — disclosed the existence of 439 heirs, scattered all over the world. Howland Bowne (and his brother, Edward), through their paternal grandmother, Elizabeth (Howland) Bowne, were fifth generation descendants of Gideon Howland and each received 1/180th of the estate, which amounted to $3,750.

Howland left the poorhouse and was able to pay some old debts, and again take up residence at the hotel. However, less than a year later, he succumbed to tuberculosis and died intestate on October 24, 1917. By this time he must have spent his modest inheritance, because his brother, Edward, paid his funeral expenses.

As we have noted earlier, Robert Bowne, the founder of Bowne & Co., had nine children, fifty grandchildren and 112 great-grandchildren. His grandson, Robert, had three sons but they all died childless and so the male line came to an end and none of the founder's hundreds of descendants alive today bears his name.

ROBERT BOWNE MINTURN (1805-1866)

Though born to a family of wealth and prominence, Robert Bowne Minturn had an early opportunity to prove his mettle. His father's successful shipping business went bankrupt at the close of the War of 1812 and Minturn, at the age of 13, had to go to work as a clerk in a New York mercantile house. He rose, however, to become one of the nation's wealthiest citizens and the swallowtail flags of the sleek Grinnell, Minturn & Co. clipper ships were to be seen on the high seas all over the world.

His most famous ship was the *Flying Cloud*. About this illustrious clipper, Henry Wadsworth Longfellow wrote these

ROBERT BOWNE MINTURN, 1805-1866, prominent New York
merchant, philanthropist and patriot of the Civil War period.

lines when he visited Donald McKay's shipyard in East Boston
in 1850:

> *Choose the timbers with greatest care;*
> *Of all that is unsound beware;*
> *For only what is sound and strong*
> *To this vessel shall belong.*
> *Cedar of Maine and Georgia pine*
> *Here together shall combine.*

Another visitor to the shipyard was Robert Bowne Minturn.
Longfellow wrote "The Building of the Ship" but Minturn was
to make that ship famous.

Enoch Train & Co. had commissioned the building of the
Flying Cloud at a cost of $45,000 and when Minturn showed
an interest in the vessel they jokingly said they would be willing to part with her for twice that figure. He promptly took them
up on the offer.

On June 3, 1851, the *Flying Cloud* weighed anchor in New
York harbor. With studding sails, royals and skysails set she
was a beautiful sight as she flashed past Sandy Hook. Despite a
terrible squall which struck her when three days out and re-
sulted in the loss of her maintopsail-yard and main and mizzen
topgallant masts, Captain Cressy would not allow any slacken-
ing of sail. This was but the first of many nerve-wracking adven-
tures the ship underwent on its voyage around Cape Horn to the
gold fields of California. During one 24-hour run, she logged
374 miles, an average of more than 15 knots.

Eighty-nine days and twenty-one hours after weighing anchor
in New York, the *Flying Cloud* went flying through the Golden

THE "FLYING CLOUD," America's most famous clipper ship
and pride of the Grinnell, Minturn & Co. fleet.

Gate to cover the sixteen thousand mile distance and to establish a record which was only broken by a British ocean-going steamship twenty-three years later.

When the *Flying Cloud* returned to New York with tea from Canton, China, she is said to have returned more than the cost of the vessel to her owners. New York went wild when she dropped anchor. Her wrecked top hamper was taken in triumph

75

to the Astor House and put on exhibit. Her log was printed on gold silk and Captain Cressy became a national hero.

The *Flying Cloud* gave the United States the honor of sailing the world's fastest ship, a prize recaptured in 1952 when the SS. *United States* broke all previous records on her maiden voyage.

Like his grandfather, Robert Bowne Minturn, was active in many philanthropic endeavors, and, at the outbreak of the Civil War, renounced those of his friends who refused to stand behind President Lincoln and organized the Union League Club, becoming its first president.

Equally famous was Minturn's partner and brother-in-law, Henry Grinnell. Long an enthusiast of Arctic exploration, he sponsored many expeditions, and when land was discovered beyond Davis Strait and Baffin Bay, it was named Grinnell Land.

The Minturns had eight children, and the Grinnells, nine. They in turn had large families and their descendants have distinguished themselves in many fields of endeavor.

RICHARD SMITH COLLINS (1825-1923)

Always to be found "in the vanguard of the great army of the Lord", Richard Smith Collins spent his almost century-long life fighting for reform. He was an Abolitionist, Prohibitionist, Suffragist, and Pacifist, never waiting for these causes to become popular, but "joining the ranks of the reformers when it cost something of scorn and derision." He and his wife, Sarah Willets Collins, were both descendants of John Bowne and their home was an important station on the "underground railway" which brought escaped slaves to safety in the North.

Both of Richard S. Collins' grandfathers were among the early printers in America. Several years before the founding of Bowne & Co., Isaac Collins was appointed the King's Printer in New Jersey. Paper currency of the day bears his imprint together with the admonition "To counterfeit is death." His was one of the first Bibles to be printed in the Colonies and was without peer for typographical accuracy. After the Revolutionary War, he came to New York and set up his publishing business in Pearl Street. The firm prided itself on never printing "novels" and other books which might be "detrimental to the morals of the community." He and his wife, Rachel Budd Collins, had fourteen children, whose average age at death was 73 years, an almost unbelievable record when compared with mortality figures for that period.

CURRENCY printed by Isaac Collins, King's Printer for New Jersey. Note the warning "To counterfeit is death."

STEPHEN WILLETS COLLINS, JR. COLLECTION

77

THE BOWNE GENEALOGY

For the interest of the descendants of Robert and Elizabeth (Hartshorne) Bowne, a genealogy of the first two generations follows.

ROBERT BOWNE (1744-1818), son of John and Dinah (Underhill) Bowne of Flushing, New York, was married in 1733 to Elizabeth Hartshorne (1750-1837), daughter of Robert and Sarah (Salter) Hartshorne of Shrewsbury, New Jersey. They had nine children:

1. MARY BOWNE (1774-1852) was married in 1794 to Benjamin Greene Minturn* (1771-1847), son of William and Penelope (Greene) Minturn of Newport, Rhode Island, and then New York City. They had eleven children:

   1. SARAH MINTURN (1795-1879) was married in 1822 to Joseph Budd Collins† (1794-1867), son of Isaac and Rachel (Budd) Collins of Burlington, New Jersey, and then New York City. They had four children, none of whom had offspring.

   2. WILLIAM H. MINTURN (1796-1853) was married in 1824 to Caroline Rebecca Byrnes (1794-1885), daughter of Joseph and Rebecca (Clarke) Byrnes of Charleston, South Carolina. They had ten children, two of whom had offspring.

   3. ELIZABETH MINTURN (1798-1823)

   4. ROBERT MINTURN (1799-1864)

---

* Benjamin G. Minturn and his brother, William, each married daughters of Robert Bowne.

† Joseph B. Collins and his brother, Benjamin, each married descendants of Robert Bowne. The former married a granddaughter and the latter, a daughter.

5. PENELOPE MINTURN (1801-1873)

6. MARY ANN MINTURN (1802-1861) was married in 1823 to Robert Hartshorne‡ (1798-1872), son of Richard and Susan (Ustick) Hartshorne of Highlands, New Jersey. They had eight children, two of whom had offspring.

7. BENJAMIN MINTURN (1803-1832)

8. JOHN CHAMPLIN MINTURN (1804-1886) was married to Sarah A. ———— (1808-1895). They had four children, none of whom had offspring.

9. EDWARD MINTURN (1806-1879)

10. CORNELIA MINTURN (1812-1882)

11. CHARLES MINTURN (1814-1873)

2. ROBERT H. BOWNE (1776-1843) was married first in 1802 to Hannah Shipley (-1805). They had two children. He was married second in 1807 to Sarah Hartshorne (1778-1861), daughter of Richard and Jane (Sayre) Hartshorne of Milford, Pennsylvania. They had six children.

Children of Robert H. and Hannah (Shipley) Bowne:

1. ROBERT S. BOWNE (1803-1830)

2. HANNAH BOWNE (1805-1812)

---

‡ There are three instances of intermarriage between the Bowne and Hartshorne families in this genealogy. The founder of the Hartshorne family was Richard Hartshorne who settled in Monmouth County, New Jersey, in 1669, where his descendants still own land which is a part of the original grant from the British Crown. Robert Bowne married Richard's great-granddaughter, Elizabeth Hartshorne. His son, Robert H. Bowne, married his own second cousin, Sarah Hartshorne. His granddaughter, Mary Ann Minturn, married Robert Hartshorne, a nephew of Elizabeth (Hartshorne) Bowne.

Children of Robert H. and Sarah (Hartshorne) Bowne:

1. RICHARD HARTSHORNE BOWNE (1810-1881) was married
   in 1837 to Emily L. Cock (1815-1888), daughter of Thomas and
   Elizabeth (Ferris) Cock of Rahway, New Jersey. They had five
   children, one of whom had offspring.

2. ELIZABETH BOWNE (1812-1882) was married in 1845 to
   Henry H. Robinson (1815-1858), son of George and Hannah
   (Phelps) Robinson of New York City. They had four children,
   none of whom had offspring.

3. HUGH HARTSHORNE BOWNE (1814-1881)

4. WILLIAM BOWNE (1816-1872)

5. JOHN L. BOWNE (1820-1894)

6. JANE BOWNE (1823-1824)

3. JOHN L. BOWNE (1779-1847) was married in 1809 to Elizabeth Howland (1792-1830), daughter of William and Abigail
   (Wilbur) Howland of New Bedford, Massachusetts. They had
   nine children:

   1. JOHN BOWNE (1810-1815)

   2. SARAH H. BOWNE (1812-1895)

   3. WILLIAM H. BOWNE (1814-1852)

   4. ELIZABETH BOWNE (1816-1909)

   5. JANE BOWNE (1818-1891) was married in 1841 to William
      Franklin Mott, Jr. (1820-1882), son of William F. and Phoebe
      (Merritt) Mott of New York City. They had four children, one
      of whom had offspring.

   6. MARY BOWNE (1820-1897)

   7. ANNA BOWNE (1822-1897)

8. ROBERT BOWNE (1825-1906) was married in 1860 to Anna Frances Willis (1834-1881), daughter of Edward and Anna (Cock) Willis of New York City. They had three children, none of whom had offspring.

9. CATHERINE BOWNE (1830-1836)

4. SARAH BOWNE (1781-1862) was married in 1800 to William Minturn, Jr. (1776-1818), son of William and Penelope (Greene) Minturn of Newport, Rhode Island, and then New York City. They had three children:

1. MARY MINTURN (1801-1856)

2. SARAH MINTURN (1803-1881) was married in 1822 to Henry Grinnell (1799-1874), son of Cornelius and Sylvia (Howland) Grinnell of New Bedford, Massachusetts. They had nine children, four of whom had offspring.

3. ROBERT BOWNE MINTURN (1805-1866) was married in 1835 to Anna Mary Wendell (1809-1886), daughter of Judge John L. and Susan (Carter) Wendell of Albany, New York. They had eight children, five of whom had offspring.

5. HANNAH BOWNE (1784-1860) was married in 1810 to Benjamin Say Collins (1784-1857), son of Isaac and Rachel (Budd) Collins of Burlington, New Jersey, and then New York City. They had ten children:

1. ELIZABETH BOWNE COLLINS (1811-1893)

2. ROBERT BOWNE COLLINS (1813-1894) was married in 1846 to Margaretta Cheeseman Murray, daughter of Lindley and Eliza (Cheeseman) Murray of New York City. They had four children, none of whom had offspring.

3. WILLIAM BOWNE COLLINS (1815-1890) was married first in 1842 to Ann Griffin (1817-1854), daughter of Solomon and Clarissa Griffin of New York City. They had three children, none of whom had offspring. He was married second in 1856 to Mary Griffin (1827-1881), sister of his first wife. They had one child, who had no offspring.

4. MARY COLLINS (1817-1826)

5. REBECCA COLLINS (1819-1901) was married in 1847 to Benjamin Tatham (1815-1885), son of James and Mary (Billington) Tatham of England. They had six children, one of whom had offspring.

6. EDWARD COLLINS (1821-1837)

7. BENJAMIN COLLINS (1822-1900)

8. RICHARD SMITH COLLINS (1825-1923) was married in 1856 to Sarah Willets (1827-1919), daughter of Stephen and Maria (Titus) Willets of New York City. They had eight children, three of whom had offspring.

9. MARY COLLINS (1828-1922)

10. CHARLES COLLINS (1830-1918)

6. ELIZABETH BOWNE (1787-1787)

7. ELIZABETH BOWNE (1789-1793)

8. JANE BOWNE (1792-1843) was married in 1812 to Reuben Haines (1786-1837), son of Caspar and Hannah (Marshall) Haines of Germantown, Pennsylvania. They had nine children:

1. SARAH MINTURN HAINES (1813-1824)

2. MARGARET HAINES (1815-1816)

3. ELIZABETH BOWNE HAINES (1817-1891) was married in 1836 to Dr. John Aston Warder (1812-1871), son of Jeremiah Warder of Springfield, Ohio. They had seven children, three of whom had offspring.

4. JOHN SMITH HAINES (1820-1886) was married in 1850 to Mary Drinker Cope (1819-1890), daughter of Henry and Rachel (Reeve) Cope of Germantown, Pennsylvania. They had three children, one of whom had offspring.

5. HANNAH HAINES (1822-1908) was married in 1843 to William Henry Bacon (1815-1882), son of John and Mary Ann (Warder) Bacon of Philadelphia, Pennsylvania. They had eleven children, five of whom had offspring.

6. SARAH HAINES (1825-1825)

7. ROBERT BOWNE HAINES (1827-1895) was married in 1852 to Margaret Vaux Wistar (1831-1917), daughter of Caspar and Lydia (Jones) Wistar of Philadelphia, Pennsylvania. They had six children, three of whom had offspring.

8. MARGARET HAINES (1830-1878) was married in 1854 to Thomas Stewardson, son of George and Rachel (Smith) Stewardson of Philadelphia, Pennsylvania. They had six children, one of whom had offspring.

9. JANE REUBEN HAINES (1832-1911)

9. WILLIAM H. BOWNE (1794-1816)